contents

4
Roast chicken

6
Chicken liver terrine

8
Warm chicken and mushroom salad

10
Chicken soup

12
Southern-fried chicken

14
Chicken chasseur

16
Deep-fried chicken with cumin and sesame

18
Cider apple chicken with mushroom sauce

20
Chicken en croûte

22
Breast of chicken with tarragon and mustard sauce

24
Coronation chicken

26
Braised chicken and coriander roulade with turmeric and almonds

28
Devilled spatchcock chickens

30
Coq au vin

32
Stuffed chicken breast with cucumber

34
Chicken Basque

36
Chicken fricassee with spring vegetables

38
Tarragon and tomato chicken casserole

40
Chicken Kiev

42
Chicken jalfrezi

44
Chicken consommé

46
Lime-marinated chicken with Mediterranean bread

48
Roasted baby chickens with herb butter

50
Smoked chicken and sun-dried tomato terrine with black olive and caper relish

52
Chicken pie

54
Chicken liver salad with bacon and croutons

56
Thai chicken wings

58
Stuffed chicken breast with celeriac purée

60
Chicken brochettes with vegetable rice

62
Chef's techniques

recipe ratings ✣ *easy* ✣✣ *a little more care needed* ✣✣✣ *more care needed*

Roast chicken

Roast chicken is an all-time favourite with many families—the tantalising smell, crisp golden skin and snowy-white flesh all add up to a traditional Sunday lunch. Use free-range for a wonderful rich flavour.

Preparation time **30 minutes**
Total cooking time **1 hour 40 minutes**
Serves 4

1 chicken, weighing 1.8 kg (3 lb 10 oz)
3 tablespoons oil
60 g (2 oz) unsalted butter
220 g (7 oz) chicken wings
1 French shallot, chopped
1 tablespoon chopped celery
1 tablespoon chopped carrot
1 tablespoon chopped onion
bouquet garni (see page 63)

1 Preheat the oven to moderately hot 200°C (400°F/ Gas 6). Truss the chicken for roasting by following the method in the Chef's techniques on page 62. Coat the bottom of a roasting tin with a tablespoon of oil. Season the chicken and rub with the remaining oil. Put the chicken on its side in the roasting tin and place the butter on top. Put in the oven and roast, basting every 5 minutes. After 15 minutes, turn the chicken onto its other side, continuing to baste every 5 minutes. After 15 minutes, turn the chicken onto its back and add the chicken wings. Roast, basting as before, for a further 20–30 minutes, or until the juices run clear.

2 Transfer the chicken and wings to an ovenproof plate, cover with foil, set aside and keep warm in a very low oven. Place the roasting tin on the stove top over low heat to clarify the fat. After 10 minutes, without stirring, the fat should be clear. Pour off the excess fat. Strain the chicken wings of excess fat and return to the roasting tin. Add the chopped vegetables and cook for 2 minutes, then add 500 ml (16 fl oz) water and the bouquet garni. Stir to loosen any bits stuck to the roasting tin, then pour into a saucepan. Bring to the boil, reduce the heat and simmer, skimming off the fat occasionally, for about 35 minutes, or until reduced in volume by three quarters. Strain and season with salt and pepper.

3 To serve, remove the string and place the chicken on a platter. Serve the roasting juices in a sauce boat.

Chef's tip To check that a chicken is cooked doesn't require any fancy gadgets or thermometers. Simply lift the chicken by inserting a carving fork into the cavity and allow the juices to drain. If the juices run clear, the chicken is cooked. If the juices have a pink tinge, give the bird another 5–10 minutes in the oven before testing it again.

Chicken liver terrine

Chicken livers have a mild flavour and soft creaminess. Take care not to overcook a terrine—this one should be moist and juicy, with the bacon wrapping adding a contrast of flavour and texture.

Preparation time 35 minutes + marinating
* + resting twice overnight*
Total cooking time 1 hour 15 minutes
Serves 4–6

20 g (³/₄ oz) unsalted butter
I small French shallot, finely chopped
185 g (6 oz) chicken livers, cut in half
315 g (10 oz) pork neck, cubed
I teaspoon brandy
I teaspoon port
¹/₈ teaspoon five-spice powder
6 rashers bacon
3 tablespoons cream
I small egg, beaten

1 Heat the butter in a pan, add the shallot and heat through for 2 minutes. Remove from the heat, add the livers and pork and stir over very low heat for 3 minutes, or until the meat and liver are warm. Mix in the brandy, port and five-spice, season well and cover with plastic wrap. Cool slightly, then refrigerate overnight.

2 Preheat the oven to very hot 250°C (500°F/Gas 10). Line a 600 ml (20 fl oz) capacity deep terrine with some of the bacon and refrigerate until ready to use. Grind the marinated livers and meat through a meat grinder set with a fine grill or in a food processor. Mix in the cream and egg, spoon into the terrine and cover with the remaining bacon.

3 Bake for 30 minutes, or until the top has begun to brown, then turn the oven to its lowest temperature. Cook for a further 30–40 minutes, or until the tip of a small knife, inserted into the centre of the terrine for a few seconds, comes out hot. Remove from the oven and allow to cool for 20 minutes. Cut a piece of cardboard or wood to just smaller than the tin and cover with foil. Place this directly onto the terrine (inside the edge of the tin), weigh down with heavy cans and refrigerate for 8 hours or overnight.

4 To unmould, first loosen the edges with a knife and then place the terrine in hot water for 30 seconds. Turn over onto a serving dish and lift away the terrine. Slice and serve with small gherkins and salad.

Warm chicken and mushroom salad

The warmth of the chicken and mushroom brings out the tangy flavour of the Dijon dressing.

*Preparation time **20 minutes***
*Total cooking time **15 minutes***
Serves 4

2 skinless chicken breast fillets
oil, for cooking
40 g (1 1/4 oz) unsalted butter
200 g (6 1/2 oz) mixed wild mushrooms, trimmed
1 French shallot, finely chopped
240 g (7 1/2 oz) mixed salad leaves
2 teaspoons Dijon mustard
2 teaspoons red wine vinegar
100 ml (3 1/4 fl oz) olive oil
sprigs of fresh chervil, to garnish

1 Season the chicken breasts, then heat a little oil in a pan and fry for 4 minutes on each side, or until tender. Remove from the pan, cover with foil and set aside.
2 Heat a little more oil in the pan, add the butter and fry the mushrooms for 3–5 minutes, or until tender and lightly coloured. Add the shallot and cook for 1 minute. Season to taste and remove with a slotted spoon.
3 Wash and dry the salad leaves and tear into bite-sized pieces. Set aside in a large bowl. Remove the foil from the chicken and slice at an angle lengthways.
4 Whisk together the mustard and vinegar. Continue whisking and slowly add the oil. Pour half the dressing over the salad leaves and toss well; place a mound in the centre of each plate. Toss the mushrooms in half the remaining dressing and sprinkle over the salad. Arrange the chicken on top. Drizzle with the remaining dressing and garnish with sprigs of fresh chervil.

LE CORDON BLEU
HOME COLLECTION
·CHICKEN·

MURDOCH BOOKS®

Sydney • London • Vancouver • New York

Chicken soup

There are few dishes as comforting as chicken soup—serve with crusty bread for instant inner warmth. This one, with its mirepoix of tiny chopped vegetables, is elegant enough for dinner with guests.

Preparation time 1 hour
Total cooking time 2 hours 15 minutes
Serves 4–6

1 chicken, weighing 1.8 kg (3 lb 10 oz), trussed (see page 62)
8 large chicken wings, cut into quarters
1 carrot, quartered lengthways
1 onion, quartered
1 leek, quartered lengthways
1 celery stick, halved
bouquet garni (see page 63)
1 teaspoon salt
60 g (2 oz) leeks
90 g (3 oz) carrots
60 g (2 oz) turnips
60 g (2 oz) celery
250 g (8 oz) potatoes
60 g (2 oz) peas
60 g (2 oz) green beans
60 g (2 oz) cabbage
60 g (2 oz) unsalted butter

1 Place the chicken and wings in a large stockpot and cover with 6 litres water. Bring to the boil, reduce the heat and simmer for 10 minutes, skimming off any fat. Add the quartered carrot, onion, leek, halved celery, bouquet garni and salt and simmer for 35 minutes. Remove the chicken and cool. Increase the heat and boil the liquid for 30 minutes. Strain and set the stock aside.

2 Meanwhile, dice the remaining vegetables to approximately the same size as the peas, keeping them separate. Melt the butter in a large stockpot. Add the leek, carrot, turnip and celery and cook slowly for 5 minutes with a pinch of salt, being careful not to allow to colour. Add the potato with a pinch of salt and cook gently for 5 minutes. Add 2 litres of the chicken stock and simmer for 15 minutes, skimming the fat and foam from the surface.

3 Blanch separately the peas, green beans and cabbage in boiling salted water for 5 minutes each. Refresh in iced water, drain and add to the soup. Simmer for a further 15 minutes, or until the vegetables are tender.

4 Remove the skin from the cooled chicken and dice the meat. Add to the soup and simmer for 5 minutes. Check the seasoning and serve.

Southern-fried chicken

Crumbed chicken, fried to crisp perfection—this is one of the classic dishes from the Deep South of America. A great family favourite for eating with your fingers.

*Preparation time **1 hour + marinating***
*Total cooking time **1 hour***
Serves 4

1 chicken, weighing 1.6 kg (3 lb 3¹/2 oz)
1.2 litres buttermilk
2 tablespoons Tabasco
170 g (5¹/2 oz) plain flour
1 teaspoon paprika
1 teaspoon dried oregano
1 teaspoon salt
¹/2 teaspoon cayenne pepper
2 eggs
2 tablespoons oil
250 g (8 oz) fresh breadcrumbs
30 g (1 oz) unsalted butter
oil, for shallow-frying

1 Cut the chicken into eight pieces, following the method in the Chef's techniques on page 63. In a large bowl, combine the buttermilk with the Tabasco and season to taste with salt. Marinate the chicken for at least 1 hour, or preferably overnight.

2 Drain the chicken and pat dry. Mix together the flour, paprika, oregano, salt and cayenne pepper in a dish and use to coat the chicken. Shake off the excess and set the chicken aside.

3 Beat the eggs with the oil and 2 tablespoons water. Dip the chicken pieces into the egg mixture, then roll in the breadcrumbs and press well. Place on a plate lined with paper towels. Preheat the oven to slow 150°C (300°F/Gas 2).

4 Heat the butter with about 2.5 cm (1 inch) oil in a large heavy-based frying pan over medium-high heat. Add the chicken, skin-side-down, and reduce the heat to medium. Cook for about 10 minutes, or until nicely coloured. If necessary, cook in batches—do not overcrowd the pan, and leave enough space between the pieces to ensure even cooking. Turn the pieces over and cook until coloured. Transfer to a baking dish or roasting pan, cover loosely with foil and bake for 45 minutes. Drain on paper towels and serve immediately.

Chef's tip You can spice up this recipe by adding a tablespoon of curry paste to the marinade.

Chicken chasseur

This classic French pan-fried chicken with a mushroom sauce is easy to prepare and will fully satisfy any guest. The recipe may be traditional but it's also versatile—try adding onions, wild mushrooms, tomatoes, button onions or smoked bacon to the sauce. Delicious with crusty bread or roast potatoes.

*Preparation time **30 minutes***
*Total cooking time **1 hour 30 minutes***
Serves 4

1 chicken, weighing 1.2 kg (2 lb 6¹/2 oz), giblets
  optional
410 ml (13 fl oz) chicken stock (see page 62)
oil, for cooking
150 g (5 oz) button mushrooms, sliced
1 large French shallot, finely chopped
25 ml (³/4 fl oz) brandy
25 ml (³/4 fl oz) white wine
2–3 large sprigs fresh tarragon
2–3 sprigs fresh chervil

1 Preheat the oven to moderately hot 200°C (400°F/ Gas 6). Cut the chicken into four or eight pieces, following the method in the Chef's techniques on page 63, then roughly cut up the remaining carcass with a knife or kitchen scissors.

2 Put the carcass pieces and giblets, if using, into a roasting tin and roast for 25 minutes, or until browned.

Remove from the oven and add the stock. Use a wooden spoon to loosen any bits stuck to the tin and simmer gently on the stove top for 30 minutes. Strain and reserve the liquid. Skim off any excess fat.

3 On the stove top, heat a little oil in the roasting tin, add the chicken pieces, skin-side-down, and brown quickly and lightly on both sides. Transfer to the oven to finish cooking: the legs will need 20 minutes, the breast and wings 15 minutes. Check that the chicken is cooked by piercing with a fork or fine skewer—the juices should run clear. Remove from the tin and keep warm.

4 Pour the excess fat from the tin, leaving 1 tablespoon and any chicken juices. Reheat on top of the stove, then add the mushrooms and cook until lightly coloured. Add the shallot and cook without browning. Increase the heat if necessary and, when the tin is very hot, add the brandy. Bring to the boil and light with a match to flambé. Add the white wine and reduce the heat to simmer for 1–2 minutes, or until reduced by half. Add the reserved chicken stock and reduce for 4–5 minutes. Season to taste with salt and pepper. Finely chop the herbs and add to the sauce—do not allow to boil again. Spoon over the chicken to serve.

Deep-fried chicken with cumin and sesame

Sesame seeds for crisp crunchy batter and a tangy dipping sauce for an eastern twist.

Preparation time **20 minutes**
Total cooking time **20 minutes**
Serves 4

80 g (2³/4 oz) plain flour
60 g (2 oz) potato flour
1 teaspoon baking powder
2 teaspoons oil
90 g (3 oz) sesame seeds
1/4 teaspoon ground cumin
3 small skinless chicken breast fillets
oil, for deep-frying

DIPPING SAUCE
1/2 teaspoon grated fresh ginger
1 teaspoon finely chopped spring onion
1 tablespoon vinegar
1 tablespoon soy sauce
2 tablespoons tomato ketchup
1 teaspoon sesame oil

1 Sift together the flour, potato flour, baking powder and a good pinch of salt into a bowl. Add the oil and whisk while adding 150 ml (5 fl oz) water in a steady stream. Whisk until the batter is smooth, add the sesame seeds and cumin and cover with plastic wrap.
2 To make the dipping sauce, mix together all the ingredients and set aside.
3 Trim the chicken of excess fat and cut lengthways into thin strips. Season, dip in the batter and deep-fry in moderately hot oil at 190°C (375°F) until golden. Drain on paper towels and serve immediately with the dipping sauce.

Cider apple chicken with mushroom sauce

The traditional French name for this recipe is Poulet Vallée d'Auge. The Auge valley
is in Normandy and this recipe makes good use of local ingredients: butter, Calvados, cider,
cream and apples from the dairy farms and apple orchards.

Preparation time 25 minutes
Total cooking time 1 hour
Serves 4

1 chicken, weighing 1.8 kg (3 lb 10 oz)
60 g (2 oz) unsalted butter
oil, for cooking
60 ml (2 fl oz) Calvados
2 French shallots, finely chopped
500 ml (16 fl oz) cider
150 g (5 oz) button mushrooms, sliced
250 ml (8 fl oz) thick (double) cream
200 g (6 1/2 oz) apples (Golden delicious)
50 g (1 3/4 oz) clarified butter (see Chef's tip)
4 tablespoons chopped fresh parsley

1 Cut the chicken into four or eight pieces, following the method in the Chef's techniques on page 63, and season with salt and pepper. Heat half the butter and a little oil in a pan and sauté the chicken in batches, skin-side-down, until lightly browned. Pour off the excess fat, return all the chicken to the pan, add the Calvados and light with a match to flambé (keep a saucepan lid on one side in case of emergency). Add the shallots and cook gently until softened but not brown. Add the cider, cover and cook for 15 minutes, turning the chicken after 10 minutes.

2 Meanwhile, sauté the mushrooms in the remaining butter, covered, for 4 minutes. Add the mushrooms and cooking juices, and the cream to the chicken and cook for 5 minutes. Remove the chicken and keep warm.

3 Continue cooking the sauce for 10 minutes, or until it is reduced enough to coat the back of a spoon. Adjust the seasoning to taste. Return the chicken to the pan, bring to the boil, reduce the heat and simmer for 2 minutes to heat the chicken through.

4 Core the unpeeled apples and cut across into thin slices. Fry in clarified butter until golden brown on both sides. Garnish the chicken with the apples and parsley.

Chef's tip Clarified butter is used because it will cook at a higher temperature without burning. You will need 90 g (3 oz) butter to yield 50 g (1 3/4 oz) clarified butter. Melt the butter gently over low heat in a small heavy-based pan, without stirring or shaking the pan. Skim the froth from the top, then carefully pour the clear butter into another container, leaving the white sediment in the base of the pan. Cover and keep in the refrigerator for up to 4 weeks.

Chicken en croûte

Succulent chicken breasts, married with mushrooms and bacon and encased in crisp plaited pastry. This dish requires a little patience in the making, but the results are spectacular.

Preparation time **1 hour + 40 minutes chilling**
Total cooking time **1 hour 30 minutes**
Serves 4

oil, for cooking
4 skinless chicken breast fillets
30 g (1 oz) unsalted butter
1 French shallot, finely chopped
1 clove garlic, finely chopped
250 g (8 oz) cup or flat mushrooms, finely chopped
400 g (12³/4 oz) block puff pastry
4 thin rashers smoked back bacon or pancetta, rind removed
1 egg, lightly beaten

SAUCE
4 chicken wings, roughly chopped
1 onion, finely chopped
2 carrots, finely chopped
1 celery stick, finely chopped
1 mushroom, finely chopped
1 bay leaf
1 tablespoon sherry vinegar
100 ml (3¹/4 oz) Madeira or sherry
500 ml (16 fl oz) chicken or beef stock (see page 62)

1 Heat about 3 tablespoons oil in a frying pan and fry the chicken for 1 minute on each side to seal. Remove from the pan and set aside.

2 Heat the butter in a medium-sized saucepan, add the shallot and garlic, cover with greaseproof paper and a lid and cook very gently until transparent and soft. Add the mushrooms and increase the heat. The mushrooms will produce juice, so cook uncovered until dry. Season with salt and pepper, then transfer to a plate to cool.

3 Cut the pastry into quarters. Roll out each piece on a lightly floured surface to a 16 x 25 cm (6¹/2 x 10 inch) rectangle. Transfer to a lightly floured baking tray and chill for 20 minutes. Slide off the tray onto a lightly floured work surface and make cuts at 2 cm (3/4 inch) intervals down the two short sides of each rectangle. Make the cuts 8 cm (3 inches) long, towards the centre of the rectangle.

4 Place a chicken breast down the centre of each pastry rectangle. Put a quarter of the mushroom mixture on each chicken breast and lightly flatten, then cover with bacon or pancetta, folding round to hold the mushroom in place. Brush the pastry strips with egg. Take the top strip of pastry from one side and place over the chicken. Take the top strip from the other side and place on top, as if to plait. Continue down the chicken, overlapping slightly and leaving small gaps between the plaiting to let the steam escape and the pastry crisp. Trim the strips at the base of the chicken or tuck underneath. Place on a buttered baking tray and chill for 20 minutes. Preheat the oven to moderately hot 200°C (400°F/Gas 6).

5 To make the sauce, add about 3 tablespoons oil to a roasting tin and heat on top of the stove. Add the wings and bake for 30 minutes, or until golden brown. Transfer to the stove top, add the chopped vegetables, bay leaf and vinegar and simmer for 5 minutes, or until reduced by three quarters and the pan juices are sticky. Add the Madeira or sherry and bring to the boil, add the stock, reduce the heat and simmer gently for 10 minutes, or until reduced by half. Skim frequently with a spoon. Strain into a clean pan and season to taste.

6 Brush the pastry parcels with egg, avoiding the cut edges or they will not rise. Bake for 25–30 minutes, or until golden and crisp. If the underside is not crisp, cover the top with foil and cook a little longer. Serve with the sauce and steamed asparagus spears.

Breast of chicken with tarragon and mustard sauce

French tarragon (as opposed to its coarser cousin, Russian tarragon) has a subtle anise-like flavour, which perfectly complements other gently flavoured foods such as eggs, fish and chicken. The Latin name means 'little dragon', from the belief that the herb could cure the bites of venomous creatures.

*Preparation time **15 minutes***
*Total cooking time **50 minutes***
Serves 4

oil, for cooking
4 skinless chicken breasts
4 French shallots, finely sliced
100 ml (3¼ fl oz) dry white wine
500 ml (16 fl oz) chicken stock (see page 62)
200 ml (6½ fl oz) thick (double) cream or crème
  fraîche
80 g (2¾ oz) Dijon or tarragon mustard
15 g (½ oz) fresh tarragon

1 Preheat the oven to moderate 180°C (350°F/Gas 4). Heat about 1 tablespoon oil in a roasting tin on the stove top and fry the chicken breasts for 5 minutes on each side, or until golden brown. Transfer to the oven and cook for a further 5–10 minutes, or until the juices run clear when a skewer is inserted into the centre.

2 Remove the chicken from the tin and keep warm. Tip off the excess fat and transfer the roasting tin to the stove top. Add the shallots and fry until soft and lightly browned, then add the wine and reduce until almost dry. Add the stock and simmer for 5–10 minutes, or until syrupy.

3 Strain the sauce into a clean pan, add the cream and simmer for 5 minutes. Stir in the mustard and season with salt and pepper, to taste. Chop the tarragon and sprinkle into the sauce at the last minute to prevent it discolouring. Serve the sauce over the chicken.

Chef's tip The shallots, which have a lovely flavour, could be left in the sauce. If you wish to do this, simply add the cream without straining the sauce first.

Coronation chicken

Originally created by Rosemary Hume of The Cordon Bleu Cookery School, London,
for the foreign dignitaries at the coronation luncheon of Queen Elizabeth II, this dish now appears on menus
around the world. Here is an updated version of the traditional recipe.

*Preparation time **30 minutes + cooling***
*Total cooking time **1 hour***
Serves 4

I chicken, weighing 1.5 kg (3 lb)
I carrot, sliced
I onion, halved
bouquet garni (see page 63)
6 peppercorns
oil, for cooking
2 French shallots, finely chopped
I teaspoon curry powder
2 teaspoons tomato paste
60 ml (2 fl oz) red wine
pinch of sugar
I slice lemon
few drops of lemon juice
I tablespoon mango chutney
220 g (7 oz) mayonnaise
3–4 tablespoons lightly whipped cream
chopped spring onion, to garnish

1 Place the chicken, carrot, onion, bouquet garni, peppercorns and a pinch of salt in a pan, add enough water to cover and bring to the boil. Reduce the heat and simmer for about 40 minutes, or until tender. Leave the chicken to cool in the liquid. When cold, remove the chicken and discard the skin and bones. Cut the chicken meat into bite-sized pieces and set aside.

2 Heat a little oil in a large saucepan, add the shallot and cook gently for 3–4 minutes. Add the curry powder and continue to cook for 1–2 minutes. Add the tomato paste, wine and 2 tablespoons water and bring to the boil. Add the sugar, salt and pepper, to taste, and the lemon and lemon juice. Reduce the heat and simmer for 5–10 minutes, or until reduced by half. Stir in the mango chutney, strain and cool.

3 Once the mixture has cooled, gradually add to the mayonnaise, to taste. Adjust the seasoning, adding a little more lemon juice if necessary. Stir in the whipped cream and chicken. Garnish with a little spring onion. Delicious served with rice salad.

Chef's tip For a rice salad that is perfect to serve with Coronation chicken, mix together 185 g (6 oz) cooked rice with cubes of cooked carrot, strips of red capsicum, sliced celery, cooked peas and peeled, seeded and quartered tomatoes. Whisk together oil and vinegar and toss over the salad, to moisten.

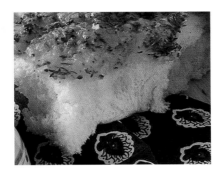

Braised chicken and coriander roulade with turmeric and almonds

This clever technique is so simple—the chicken breast is cut open then rolled around the fresh coriander. After cooking, the roll is sliced to reveal a colourful, moist filling.

*Preparation time **30 minutes***
*Total cooking time **15 minutes***
Serves 4

4 skinless chicken breast fillets, weighing
   150 g (5 oz) each
30 g (1 oz) fresh coriander leaves
oil, for cooking
1 tablespoon ground turmeric
500 ml (16 fl oz) chicken stock (see page 62)
100 g (3 1/4 oz) whole blanched almonds

1 Preheat the oven to moderately hot 200°C (400°F/ Gas 6). Lay the chicken breasts flat on a cutting board, putting a hand flat on top to gently hold the meat in place. Slice into the side of each breast until you have cut two thirds across, then open the breast like a book. Place a layer of coriander on top of each breast, reserving some to garnish, and season with salt and pepper. Roll up the breasts from the bottom to enclose the coriander and secure the rolls with string.

2 Heat 2–3 tablespoons oil in a heavy-based flameproof casserole over high heat. When very hot, add the chicken rolls and brown quickly on all sides. Remove the chicken from the pan, pour off the oil and add the turmeric. Return the chicken rolls to the pan and shake until they are well coated with turmeric. Add the stock and bring to the boil. Add the almonds, cover and place the casserole in the oven for 8–10 minutes, or until the rolls have cooked through.

3 Remove the rolls from the liquid, cover to prevent drying out and leave in a warm place. Strain the cooking liquid. Place the almonds in a blender or food processor, add 100 ml (3 1/4 fl oz) of the cooking liquid and purée until smooth. Gradually add more of the liquid and process until the sauce has a flowing consistency. Season to taste with salt and pepper.

4 Remove the string and cut across the chicken rolls into six slices each. Arrange the slices on a hot plate and pour some sauce around. Garnish with coriander leaves to serve.

Devilled spatchcock chickens

The name spatchcock derives from medieval times, when a traveller would arrive late at an inn and a bird would be quickly 'despatched' and roasted.

Preparation time **30 minutes**
Total cooking time **1 hour**
Serves 4

4 baby chickens, about 440 g (14 oz) each
melted butter or oil, for cooking
60 g (2 oz) Dijon or English mustard
60 g (2 oz) fresh breadcrumbs
chopped fresh parsley, to garnish

1 Remove the wishbones from the chickens, following the method in the Chef's techniques on page 63, and preheat the oven to moderate 180°C (350°F/Gas 4).
2 To open and flatten the chickens, rinse out the inside cavity, then with the breast-side-down, use kitchen scissors to cut along each side of the backbone and remove it. Turn the chickens breast-side-up and push down with the weight of two flat hands to break the breastbone. Tuck the pointed end wing joints under the breast. Run a skewer between the two bones of one of the middle wing joints, then through the breast and out through to the wing on the other side. Push another metal skewer through from one thigh to the other. Lay the chickens flat, breast-side-up, on an oiled baking tray.
3 Brush with the butter or oil and season lightly. Place under a low grill to lightly colour, then roast in the oven for 40–50 minutes, or until the juices run clear.
4 Spread the chicken skin evenly with the mustard, sprinkle with breadcrumbs, then drizzle with a little melted butter or oil. Place under a hot grill until golden brown and garnish with parsley to serve.

Coq au vin

The long list of ingredients is not as daunting as it appears. The chicken is marinated overnight in wine, vegetables and herbs to tenderise and flavour it, and the dish can quickly be put together the next day. This traditional recipe originated in the Burgundy region, famous for its fine red wines.

Preparation time **50 minutes + overnight marinating**
Total cooking time **2 hours**
Serves 6–8

MARINADE
I onion, chopped
I carrot, chopped
5 juniper berries
10 peppercorns
I clove
I clove garlic
2 litres red wine
50 ml (1³/4 fl oz) Cognac
30 ml (1 fl oz) red wine vinegar
bouquet garni (see page 63)

3 kg (6 lb) chicken pieces
clarified butter or oil, for cooking
45 g (1¹/2 oz) plain flour
800 ml (26 fl oz) chicken stock (see page 62)
185 g (6 oz) smoked streaky bacon
200 g (6¹/2 oz) pearl onions
20 g (³/4 oz) caster sugar
20 g (³/4 oz) unsalted butter
150 g (5 oz) button mushrooms

CROUTONS
4 slices bread, crusts removed
150 ml (5 fl oz) clarified butter or oil
I tablespoon chopped fresh parsley

1 To make the marinade, place all the ingredients into a large non-metallic bowl. Add the chicken pieces, cover and leave overnight in the refrigerator.

2 Remove the chicken and dry with paper towels. Strain the marinade and reserve the vegetables and herbs separately from the liquid. Preheat the oven to moderately hot 200°C (400°F/Gas 6).

3 Heat a little clarified butter or oil in a deep flameproof casserole dish and sauté the chicken over high heat, skin-side-down first, until well browned on all sides. Add the reserved marinade vegetables and herbs. Cook for 5 minutes, or until softened, stirring occasionally. Pour off any excess fat. Sprinkle the flour into the dish and mix well. Add the reserved marinade, hot stock and salt and pepper. Cover with greaseproof paper and a lid and cook in the oven for 45 minutes, or until the chicken is cooked through. Reduce the oven temperature to low. Remove the chicken to a clean casserole, strain the sauce and skim off the excess fat. Season if necessary. Pour over the chicken and return to the oven to heat through.

4 Meanwhile, put the bacon in a pan, cover with water and bring to the boil. Drain, rinse under cold water and trim away the rind. Cut into small pieces and fry in a little oil until golden; drain on paper towels. Put the onions, sugar and butter in a pan with just enough water to cover. Bring to the boil, then simmer until all the water has evaporated and the onions are tender (if necessary, add a little extra water and continue cooking). Glaze the onions by tossing in the butter and sugar in the pan until golden. Fry the mushrooms in hot oil and drain. Sprinkle the bacon, onions and mushrooms over the chicken, cover and keep warm.

5 To make croutons, cut each slice of bread into four triangles and fry in very hot clarified butter or oil until golden brown—be careful as the bread colours quickly. Dip the tips of the croutons in the parsley and arrange over the dish.

Stuffed chicken breast with cucumber

The cucumber's origins date back to Roman times and with its cool and refreshing qualities it is included in many of today's recipes. This dish is beautifully light and brings a taste of summer all year round.

Preparation time **35 minutes + 20 minutes chilling**
Total cooking time **40 minutes**
Serves 6

1 chicken Maryland (leg quarter), skinned
1 egg white
185 ml (6 fl oz) thick (double) cream
30 g (1 oz) chopped mixed fresh herbs
6 skinless chicken breast fillets, about 185 g (6 oz)
each
1 telegraph cucumber
3 French shallots, finely chopped
100 ml (3¼ fl oz) dry white wine
500 ml (16 fl oz) chicken stock (see page 62)
410 ml (13 fl oz) thick (double) cream, extra

1 Cut the flesh from the chicken maryland, scraping it from the bone, and purée in a food processor. Lightly beat the egg white and add just over half of it to the chicken (discard the remainder). Season with salt and pepper, then use the pulse button to mix in the cream and herbs. Do not overprocess or the cream may split. Cover and chill for 15–20 minutes to firm up slightly.

2 Remove the thin fillets (tenderloins) from the underside of the chicken breasts and place on lightly oiled plastic wrap or greaseproof paper. Gently flatten them with a cutlet bat or small heavy-based pan and store in the refrigerator.

3 Make a short slit on the top of each chicken breast and make a pocket by cutting just under either side of the slit with the tip of a small sharp knife. Using a spoon or piping bag, fill each pocket with the prepared chicken purée; do not overfill or it will burst its shape in cooking. Place a flattened fillet over the top of each chicken breast to completely cover the chicken purée. Wrap each breast in buttered foil, twisting the ends tightly to seal. Poach in gently simmering water for 20–30 minutes. Remove from the heat and leave to rest in the hot poaching liquid.

4 Cut the unpeeled cucumber in half lengthways and, using the point of a teaspoon, scrape out the seeds. Cut three quarters of the cucumber into 5 cm (2 inch) lengths and cut into strips about the thickness of a little finger. Blanch in a small pan of boiling salted water for 2–3 minutes, rinse under cold water and drain. Roughly chop the remaining cucumber and set aside.

5 To make the sauce, place the shallots, wine and chicken stock in a wide pan and quickly bring to the boil. Boil the sauce for 5 minutes, or until it has reduced to a light syrupy consistency. Add the extra cream and boil until the mixture thickens slightly. Add the chopped cucumber and boil for a further 5 minutes. Transfer the sauce to a blender or food processor and purée well. Season with salt and pepper and strain through a sieve.

6 Serve the chicken breasts immediately, either whole or sliced, with the cucumber strips and sauce.

Chicken Basque

The Basque country is located in the south-west of France and northern Spain, close to the Pyrenees mountains. This traditional recipe uses local produce such as onions, capsicums, tomatoes and garlic but we have substituted the more readily available Parma ham or prosciutto for the local cured ham from Bayonne, and olive oil instead of the traditional goose fat.

Preparation time **30 minutes**
Total cooking time **1 hour 15 minutes**
Serves 4

2 red capsicums (peppers)
2 green capsicums (peppers)
410 g (13 oz) tomatoes
1 chicken, weighing 1.2 kg (2 lb 6¹/2 oz)
oil, for cooking
1 large onion, finely sliced
3 cloves garlic, crushed
100 ml (3¹/4 fl oz) white wine
90 g (3 oz) Parma ham or prosciutto, cut into strips
1 tablespoon chopped fresh parsley, to garnish

1   Halve the capsicums, remove the seeds and membrane and slice the flesh into long strips. Score a cross in the base of each tomato, then plunge into boiling water for 10 seconds. Rinse with cold water and peel the skin away from the cross. Quarter and remove the seeds.

2   Cut the chicken into eight pieces, following the method in the Chef's techniques on page 63. Season with salt and pepper. Heat about 2 tablespoons oil in a large deep frying pan. Add the chicken pieces, skin-side-down first, and fry until lightly golden brown all over. Remove and drain on crumpled paper towels.

3   Tip off the excess oil, leaving just 1 tablespoon in the pan. Add the onion, garlic, capsicum and tomato and leave to simmer for 10 minutes. Add the white wine, cover and leave to simmer for a further 30 minutes. Add the chicken, season lightly with salt and pepper, cover and simmer for 15–20 minutes. Check that the chicken is fully cooked by pricking it with a fork (the juices should run clear). Lift out the chicken pieces, cover with foil and keep warm. Season the sauce with salt and pepper, to taste.

4   Pan-fry the ham or prosciutto in a little oil, lifting directly from the pan with a slotted spoon, without draining on paper towels. Pour the sauce over the chicken, sprinkle with the ham or prosciutto and garnish with the parsley.

Chicken fricassee with spring vegetables

The word fricassee is French in origin and may have been a marriage of two culinary terms: 'frire', which means to fry, and 'casse', meaning ladle or dripping pan.

*Preparation time **25 minutes***
*Total cooking time **1 hour***
*Serves **4***

1 chicken, weighing 1.8 kg (3 lb 10 oz)
30 g (1 oz) plain flour, seasoned with salt and pepper
oil, for cooking
35 g (1¼ oz) unsalted butter
6 French shallots, thinly sliced
100 ml (3¼ fl oz) dry white wine
250 ml (8 fl oz) chicken stock (see page 62)
bouquet garni (see page 63)
1 egg yolk
150 g (5 oz) sour cream
300 g (10 oz) baby carrots
300 g (10 oz) baby turnips
150 g (5 oz) large spring onions
1 teaspoon sugar
***200 g (6½ oz) snow peas (mangetout), topped and
    tailed***
250 g (8 oz) asparagus spears
100 g (3¼ oz) button mushrooms

1 Cut the chicken into eight pieces, following the method in the Chef's techniques on page 63. Coat the chicken pieces in the seasoned flour, shaking off and reserving the excess. Heat a little oil in a large frying pan over medium heat, add 15 g (1/2 oz) of the butter and cook the chicken quickly to seal without colouring; remove from the pan and set aside. Lower the heat, add the shallots to the pan and cook slowly, without colouring, until softened. Stir in the reserved flour, then pour in the wine, stirring until the mixture boils and thickens. Reduce the heat and simmer for 2 minutes, then stir in the stock and bouquet garni. Return the chicken to the pan, cover and simmer for 15 minutes. Remove the wings and breast meat, keeping them covered and warm, and cook for a further 5 minutes. Remove the chicken thighs and legs, leaving the cooking liquid in the pan.

2 Increase the heat and let the liquid boil for 5–10 minutes, or until reduced by half, skimming off the excess fat with a spoon. Mix the egg yolk with a tablespoon of sour cream in a bowl. Stir the remaining sour cream into the pan and bring to the boil, then simmer for 2 minutes. Remove from the heat, pour a little hot sauce onto the egg yolk mixture, blend and return to the pan, whisking or stirring until heated (do not allow to boil). Strain, season to taste and set aside.

3 Place the carrots, turnips and spring onions in separate small pans with just enough water to cover. Add a small pinch of salt, sugar and a third of the remaining butter to each pan, then press on buttered greaseproof paper to cover. Cook gently until the water has nearly evaporated and the vegetables are cooked and shiny, shaking the pan occasionally. Remove to a lightly buttered dish, arrange in separate piles and keep warm.

4 Cook the snow peas, asparagus and mushrooms in salted boiling water for 3–5 minutes, or until tender but still keeping a crisp bite. Drain well.

5 Arrange a piece of chicken breast and dark meat on each plate and coat with the sauce. Serve with the vegetables.

Tarragon and tomato chicken casserole

This recipe comes from Lyon, France's third largest city and its gastronomic capital, situated close to the Burgundy vineyards.

Preparation time **20 minutes**
Total cooking time **45 minutes**
Serves 4

I chicken, weighing 1.2 kg (2 lb 6¹/2 oz)
oil or butter, for cooking
200 ml (6¹/2 fl oz) tarragon vinegar (see Chef's tip)
I kg (2 lb) tomatoes
15 g (¹/2 oz) unsalted butter, softened
15 g (¹/2 oz) plain flour
sprig of fresh tarragon, to garnish

1 Cut the chicken into four or eight pieces, following the method in the Chef's techniques on page 63, and season with salt and pepper. Heat a little oil or butter in a frying pan and brown the chicken on all sides, skin-side-down first. Do not overcrowd the pan so, if necessary, brown the chicken in batches. Remove the chicken and pour off any excess oil from the pan.

2 Return all the chicken to the pan and add half of the tarragon vinegar. Cover and simmer for 10 minutes.

Turn the chicken pieces over, cover and cook for a further 10 minutes, or until the juices run clear when pricked with a fork. Remove the chicken from the pan. Cover the pan and keep the sauce warm.

3 Score a cross in the base of each tomato, then plunge into boiling water for 10 seconds. Rinse with cold water and peel the skin away from the cross. Cut in half, remove the seeds, then cut into eighths. Put the remaining vinegar in a pan and boil for 4 minutes. Mix together the softened butter and flour, whisk into the reduced vinegar and then whisk this into the sauce. Return the chicken to the sauce, add the tomato and simmer for 10 minutes, or until the sauce just coats the back of a spoon. Check the seasoning. Chop the fresh tarragon just before serving, sprinkle over the casserole and serve with rice.

Chef's tip Make your own tarragon vinegar by placing a sprig of fresh tarragon into a bottle of ordinary red or white wine vinegar. After a week, strain out the tarragon and your vinegar is ready. All your favourite herbs can be used in this way.

Chicken Kiev

You can shallow-fry or deep-fry your Chicken Kiev to produce a crisp coating for the chicken and garlic butter, which bursts with succulence and flavour as you cut into it.

*Preparation time **40 minutes***
*Total cooking time **40 minutes***
Serves 4

4 skinless chicken breasts fillets
120 g (4 oz) plain flour, seasoned with salt and pepper
3 eggs, beaten
200 g (6¹/2 oz) dried white breadcrumbs, sieved
oil, for cooking and deep-frying

GARLIC BUTTER
150 g (5 oz) unsalted butter
3 cloves garlic, crushed
50 g (1³/4 oz) chopped fresh parsley

1 Remove the thin fillets (tenderloins) from the underside of the chicken breasts and place them on lightly oiled plastic wrap or greaseproof paper. Gently flatten them with a cutlet bat or small heavy-based pan and put in the refrigerator.

2 To make the garlic butter, soften the butter, then add the garlic, parsley, salt and pepper, and mix well. Spoon the butter along one end of a piece of oiled plastic wrap or damp greaseproof paper and roll it up into a sausage shape, twisting the ends. Refrigerate until firm.

3 Cut a short slit into the top of each chicken breast and make a pocket by cutting just under either side of the slit with the tip of a small sharp knife. Carefully place a slice of the firm garlic butter into each pocket. Place a flattened fillet over the top of each chicken breast to completely cover the butter.

4 Place the seasoned flour, egg and breadcrumbs in separate shallow dishes. Coat the chicken with the flour, then with the egg and finally with the breadcrumbs. Coat again with the egg and breadcrumbs.

5 Preheat the oven to moderately hot 200°C (400°F/ Gas 6). To shallow-fry, heat enough oil in a frying pan to come halfway up the sides of the chicken. Cook the Kievs over medium heat for 6 minutes each side, or until golden brown and cooked through. Transfer to a wire rack in the oven for a few minutes to allow the coating to crisp further.

6 To deep-fry, preheat the oil in the deep fryer to moderately low 160°C (315°F). Add two of the chicken breasts and fry for about 12 minutes, or until golden brown. Remove from the oil and drain on crumpled paper towels. Keep warm in the oven on a wire rack while cooking the rest. Serve Chicken Kievs with a crisp salad and fresh bread.

Chicken jalfrezi

This spicy curry can be found under
many guises—jalfreji, jalfresi and even jhal fry.

Preparation time **20 minutes**
Total cooking time **55 minutes**
Serves 4

oil, for cooking
1 onion, finely grated
2 cloves garlic, chopped
750 g (1 1/2 lb) skinless chicken thigh fillets, cut in half
3 teaspoons ground turmeric
1 teaspoon red chilli powder
1 1/2 teaspoons salt
500 g (1 lb) can chopped tomatoes
30 g (1 oz) ghee or 2 tablespoons oil
3 teaspoons ground cumin
3 teaspoons ground coriander
2 tablespoons grated fresh ginger
30 g (1 oz) fresh coriander leaves, roughly chopped

1 Heat about 2 tablespoons oil in a deep frying pan and fry the onion and garlic for 2 minutes over high heat.
2 Add the chicken, turmeric, chilli powder and salt. Fry gently for 5–10 minutes, or until golden brown, scraping the base of the pan frequently and turning the chicken. Add the tomato, cover and cook over medium heat for 20 minutes. Uncover and simmer for 10 minutes to let all the excess liquid evaporate and the sauce thicken.
3 Add the ghee or oil, cumin, ground coriander, ginger and fresh coriander and simmer for 5–7 minutes, or until the fat separates out from the thick sauce. Season if necessary. Serve the chicken pieces with the sauce spooned on top. This dish could be served with Basmati rice, chapattis or naan bread.

Chicken consommé

A consommé is a classic clear soup made from meat, chicken or fish stock.
The name comes from the French word 'consommer', meaning to finish up or use up
and is so called because all the goodness of the meat goes into the soup.

Preparation time **45 minutes**
Total cooking time **3 hours 15 minutes**
Serves 4

1.25 kg (2 lb 8 oz) chicken legs
250 g (8 oz) lean minced beef
1 teaspoon oil
1 small carrot, roughly chopped
1 small leek, roughly chopped
1 small celery stick, roughly chopped
1 small onion, halved
2 cloves, stuck into the onion
bouquet garni (see page 63)
1 teaspoon salt
6 peppercorns
2 egg whites

TO SERVE
10 g (¹/4 oz) butter
¹/2 small leek, white part only, cut into julienne strips
  (see Chef's tips)
¹/2 small carrot, cut into julienne strips
¹/2 celery stick, cut into julienne strips

1 Preheat the oven to moderately hot 200°C (400°F/ Gas 6). Remove the skin from the chicken legs and discard. Scrape the meat from the bones, following the method in the Chef's techniques on page 63, place in a food processor and process until finely minced. Place the minced chicken and the beef in a bowl in the refrigerator. Coarsely chop the bones, place in a roasting tin and bake for 30–40 minutes, or until well browned.

2 Heat the oil in a heavy-based pan, add the carrot, leek and celery and cook until lightly coloured. Set aside. Heat a cast-iron or stainless steel pan and add the onion, cut-side-down. Cook over medium heat until the onion has blackened.

3 Place the bones, carrot, leek, celery, onion, bouquet garni, salt and peppercorns in a large stockpot and cover with 2 litres cold water. Add the egg whites to the ground meat and mix with a wooden spoon, then add 500 ml (16 fl oz) water and mix well. Add to the stockpot and mix well. Place the stockpot over medium heat and bring slowly to the boil, stirring every 2 minutes. Reduce the heat and leave to gently simmer for 2 hours. Line a fine sieve with a clean tea towel and place over a clean pan. Gently ladle the consommé into the sieve and strain into the pan.

4 To serve, melt the butter in a small frying pan. Add the julienned vegetables along with a pinch of salt and cook, covered, over low heat for 10–15 minutes, or until the vegetables are cooked but still firm. Strain and pat dry to remove the excess butter, then place in four bowls and pour in the hot consommé.

Chef's tips Julienne strips are even-sized strips of vegetables the size and shape of matchsticks. They cook quickly and are very decorative.

To remove the maximum amount of fat, the consommé is best made a day in advance and refrigerated overnight, or until the excess fat solidifies on the surface. Skim off the fat before reheating the consommé over a pan of gently simmering water.

Lime-marinated chicken with Mediterranean bread

This refreshing dish combines the flavours of the Mediterranean and the tropics. Lime, yoghurt and coriander blend especially well together and are complemented by a light, crusty bread.

Preparation time **50 minutes + rising + marinating**
Total cooking time **55 minutes**
Serves 4

MEDITERRANEAN BREAD (see Chef's tips)
440 ml (14 fl oz) lukewarm water
30 g (1 oz) fresh yeast
680 g (1 lb 6 oz) strong or unbleached flour
140 ml (4¹/₂ fl oz) extra virgin olive oil
3 teaspoons salt
100 g (3¹/₄ oz) pitted black olives, roughly chopped
100 g (3¹/₄ oz) sun-dried tomatoes, soaked, drained and roughly chopped (see Chef's tips)

410 g (13 oz) plain yoghurt
2 fresh green chillies, seeded and chopped
2 cloves garlic, chopped
3 tablespoons roughly chopped fresh coriander
grated rind of 3 limes
juice of ¹/₂ lime
8 skinless chicken thigh fillets

1 To make the Mediterranean bread, combine the warm water and yeast in a small bowl and stir together until smoothly blended. Sieve 440 g (14 oz) of the strong flour into a bowl and make a well in the centre. Pour the yeast and water into the well, followed by the olive oil. Using your hand with fingers slightly apart, gradually begin to draw the flour into the liquid in the well. Continue until all the flour has been incorporated and a loose batter is formed. Beat for 5 minutes in a slapping motion to develop its elasticity and free it from lumps. Clean the sides of the bowl with a scraper, cover with a damp cloth and leave at room temperature to rise for 1–1¹/₂ hours, or until doubled in volume. Add the remaining flour, salt, olives and sun-dried tomatoes and mix well. Scrape down the side of the bowl, cover with a fresh damp cloth and leave until doubled in volume.

2 Preheat the oven to moderately hot 200°C (400°F/ Gas 6). Lightly butter and flour two medium-sized baking trays. Divide the very soft dough in half (do not be alarmed by the very loose texture—this is quite normal). Be careful not to overhandle the dough or it will lose volume. Place on the trays and, with wet hands, gently pat and shape each piece to a rectangle about 2¹/₂ cm (1 inch) thick. Sprinkle with cold water and dust heavily with extra flour. Bake in the oven for 35–40 minutes, or until a skewer inserted into the centre of the bread comes out clean. Transfer to a cooling rack and leave for 20 minutes before serving.

3 For the marinated chicken, combine the yoghurt, chilli, garlic, coriander and lime rind and juice in a blender until smooth. Season with salt and pepper. Place half the mixture in a dish and lay the chicken on top. Cover with the remaining mixture and leave in a cool place for 30 minutes. Arrange the chicken on a baking sheet or grill pan. Grill gently, turning frequently, for up to 15 minutes, or until cooked through. Serve with the Mediterranean bread.

Chef's tips The Mediterranean bread is a perfect complement to the marinated chicken, but be sure to prepare it well in advance to give time for the dough to rise. The nature of this bread is for it to have an uneven, crusty texture. The olive oil gives the crustiness and not knocking back the dough during rising creates the holes in the loaf.

If you are using sun-dried tomatoes in oil, there is no need to soak them before draining and chopping.

Roasted baby chickens with herb butter

This is a deliciously simple variation on a plain roast chicken. Use whichever fresh herbs you have to hand and pick up the same flavours in the buttery sauce.

Preparation time **40 minutes**
Total cooking time **1 hour 15 minutes**
Serves 4

2 spring chickens, weighing 440 g (14 oz) each
90 g (3oz) unsalted butter, softened
3 tablespoons chopped mixed fresh herbs (tarragon,
  chervil, parsley)
2 tablespoons oil
3–4 chicken wings
2 tablespoons chopped carrot
2 tablespoons chopped French shallot
2 tablespoons chopped onion
I tablespoon chopped celery

1 Preheat the oven to moderately hot 200°C (400°F/ Gas 6). Prepare the chickens by gently sliding a finger under the skin at the neck end and loosening the skin from the flesh. Be careful not to tear the skin.

2 In a small bowl, mix together the butter and herbs and season to taste with salt and pepper. Using a piping bag with a small nozzle, pipe about 1 1/2 tablespoons herb butter under the skin of each chicken, using your fingers to spread out the butter as much as possible. If you do not have a piping bag, simply use the handle of a fork or spoon to spread the herb butter under the skin.

Truss the chickens for roasting, following the method in the Chef's techniques on page 62. Reserve the remaining herb butter for the sauce.

3 Heat a roasting tin on the stove top over medium-low heat. Add the oil and place the chickens on their side in the tin. Once the oil is hot, place the roasting tin in the oven and roast the chickens for 10 minutes, basting every 5 minutes. Turn the chickens onto their other side and roast for 10 minutes, basting every 5 minutes. Turn the chickens onto their backs, add the chicken wings and roast for 10 minutes, or until the chicken juices run clear, basting every 5 minutes.

4 Transfer the chicken and wings to an ovenproof plate, cover with foil and keep warm in a very low oven. Place the roasting tin on the stove top over low heat to clarify the fat, if necessary. After 5–10 minutes, without stirring, the fat should be clear. Strain the chicken wings of excess fat and return to the roasting tin. Add the vegetables and cook for 2 minutes, then add 500 ml (16 fl oz) water. Stir to loosen the cooking juices from the roasting tin, then pour into a saucepan. Bring to the boil, then reduce the heat to simmer, skimming off the fat. Simmer for 35 minutes, or until reduced by three quarters. Strain into a smaller saucepan, discarding the chicken wings. Whisk in the remaining herb butter, season and pour into a sauce boat. Remove the string and cut the chickens in half. Serve with the sauce.

Smoked chicken and sun-dried tomato terrine with black olive and caper relish

Terrines are an impressive and elegant way to dress your dinner or buffet table, but a few slices served with a salad would also make an ideal first course or lunch.

Preparation time **1 hour 20 minutes + overnight refrigeration if possible**
Total cooking time **1 hour 30 minutes**
Serves 12

I smoked chicken, weighing about I kg (2 lb)
4 large chicken legs
2 egg whites
300 ml (10 fl oz) thick (double) cream
100 g (3 1/4 oz) sun-dried tomatoes, shredded
100 g (3 1/4 oz) mixed fresh herbs, chopped

BLACK OLIVE AND CAPER RELISH
100 g (3 1/4 oz) pitted black olives, sliced
100 g (3 1/4 oz) capers, roughly chopped
I clove garlic, chopped
30 g (I oz) fresh chives, chopped
3 teaspoons olive oil

1 With a sharp knife, cut down each side of the breastbone of the smoked chicken, remove the wings and set aside the two breast pieces. Remove the skin and cut away the leg meat from the chicken, discarding the bones. Mince or finely chop the leg meat in a food processor and set aside.

2 With a small sharp knife scrape the flesh from the raw chicken legs, following the method in the Chef's techniques on page 63. Trim away the fine, shiny, white nerves and tendons—these will not break down during cooking and will spoil the smooth texture of the terrine.

Work the raw meat to a fine purée in the food processor, then blend in the egg whites. Transfer to a bowl, cover and refrigerate for 15 minutes. Preheat the oven to warm 160°C (315°F/Gas 2–3).

3 Sit the bowl of puréed chicken over ice and slowly mix in the cream to just blend. Season with salt and pepper. Gently mix in the smoked leg meat, sun-dried tomatoes and herbs.

4 Line the length of the base of a 1.5 litre capacity terrine with a strip of doubled greaseproof paper or foil, to overhang the sides and help you unmould the terrine after cooking. Half-fill the terrine with the chicken mixture, place the smoked chicken breasts on top and cover with the remaining chicken mixture. Cover the terrine with foil, firmly turning under to seal the edges.

5 Place the terrine in an ovenproof dish and create a water bath by pouring in hand-hot water to come halfway up the outside of the mould. Bake in the oven for 1 1/2 hours, or until the juices run clear when tested with a skewer. Remove from the water bath and leave to cool in the mould. The terrine is best left refrigerated overnight to make slicing easier.

6 To make the relish, mix the olives with the capers, garlic and chives, then stir in the olive oil to bind. Loosen the edges of the terrine with a sharp knife, then turn out and cut into 12 slices. Serve with the relish.

Chef's tip In step 3, it is very important that the cream and meat purée be chilled. If not, there is a risk of the cream splitting. If the cream splits, the smooth light texture of the terrine is spoiled.

Chicken pie

*Serve this delicious pie with simple boiled or creamed potatoes to mop up the chicken juices.
Brussels sprouts or spinach would also be delicious accompaniments.
Alternatively, for a crisper bite, serve with a mixed green side salad.*

Preparation time **45 minutes + 30 minutes resting**
Total cooking time **1 hour 35 minutes**
Serves **4–6**

1 chicken, weighing 1.5 kg (3 lb)
8 slices pancetta, about 185 g (6 oz), rind removed
60 g (2 oz) unsalted butter
1 hard-boiled egg, roughly chopped
100 g (3¼ oz) button mushrooms, quartered
1 onion, finely chopped
60 ml (2 fl oz) white wine
250 ml (8 fl oz) chicken stock (see page 62)
250 g (8 oz) ready-made puff pastry
1 egg, beaten
*good pinch of chopped fresh herbs, such as parsley,
    tarragon or chervil*

1 Cut the chicken into eight pieces, following the method in the Chef's techniques on page 63, and remove the bones and skin. Season with salt and pepper, then wrap each piece of chicken in a slice of pancetta and secure with cocktail sticks or string.

2 Heat half the butter in a frying pan over medium heat and lightly brown the chicken in batches, turning regularly to seal on all sides. Remove the chicken from the pan and drain on crumpled paper towels. Discard the cocktail sticks or string and place the chicken in a 1.5 litre capacity pie dish with the hard-boiled egg. Pour off the excess fat from the pan, add the remaining butter and cook the mushrooms and onion over low heat for 5 minutes without colouring.

3 Add the white wine to the pan and simmer until only a little liquid is left. Pour over the chicken in the dish. Add sufficient stock to almost cover the chicken pieces.

4 Roll out the pastry so that it is a little bigger than the top of the dish. Brush the rim of the pie dish with beaten egg and line with 1 cm (1/2 inch) of spare pastry cut from around the pastry edge, pressing onto the dish firmly and brushing with beaten egg. Fold the pastry over a rolling pin and cover the pie dish. Be careful not to stretch the pastry or it will shrink out of shape while baking. Press the edges together to seal. With a small sharp knife, trim off the excess pastry. Do not angle the knife in towards the dish or it will encourage shrinkage later. With the back of the knife, notch the cut pastry edge. Brush the top surface with egg, but not the edges. Make a small hole for steam to escape, then decorate with pastry trimmings and brush them with egg.

5 Chill the pie for 30 minutes, to prevent it shrinking during baking, and preheat the oven to moderately hot 190°C (375°F/Gas 5). Bake the pie for 20 minutes, or until the pastry is risen and golden. Reduce the oven to very slow 120°C (250°F/Gas 1/2) and cover the pie with foil to prevent overbrowning while cooking the chicken through. Cook for 45 minutes. Break the crust in the centre, or loosen and lift off from the side, and add the chopped fresh herbs. Serve immediately.

Chef's tip This pie traditionally has a lot of thin gravy, delicious mopped up with potatoes. If you prefer a thicker sauce, chop up the mushrooms more finely, or roll the chicken pieces in seasoned flour after sealing and before putting in the pie dish.

Chicken liver salad with bacon and croutons

Chicken liver has a delicate flavour and soft moist texture when cooked. When pan-fried it is best served slightly pink in the centre. Here, the sherry vinegar dressing cuts its richness.

Preparation time **15 minutes**
Total cooking time **15 minutes**
Serves 4

345 g (11 oz) mixed salad leaves
200 g (6¹/₂ oz) smoked bacon, rind removed, cut into thin strips
100 ml (3¹/₄ fl oz) oil
2 slices bread, crusts removed, cut into small cubes
440 g (14 oz) chicken livers
30 g (1 oz) unsalted butter
3 French shallots, finely chopped
2 tablespoons vinegar

VINAIGRETTE DRESSING
1¹/₂ tablespoons Dijon mustard
3 tablespoons sherry vinegar
100 ml (3¹/₄ fl oz) oil

1 Wash and dry the salad leaves and then refrigerate, covered with a tea towel, to prevent wilting.

2 Fry the bacon in a dry pan over medium heat. Lift out and drain on crumpled paper towels. Set aside.

3 Heat the oil in a shallow pan, add the bread cubes and fry, stirring, until golden brown. Lift out and drain on crumpled paper towels. Sprinkle lightly with salt and keep warm.

4 Clean the chicken livers, removing the small green area that can be bitter, and cut into small pieces. Heat the butter in a shallow pan and toss the liver over high heat for 2 minutes. Add the shallots and fry for a further 2 minutes, then season with salt and pepper and transfer to a plate. The liver should be barely pink and juicy inside. Add the vinegar to the pan and heat to dissolve any sticky juices. Pour over the liver and keep warm.

5 To make the vinaigrette dressing, put the mustard, sherry vinegar and salt and pepper to taste in a bowl and add the oil in a slow, steady stream, mixing continuously with a fork or small whisk until fully blended.

6 Put the salad leaves in a bowl, pour over the dressing and carefully toss to coat thoroughly without bruising the leaves. Serve topped with the bacon, croutons and liver with its juices.

Thai chicken wings

*These crisp-skinned wings have the intense Thai
flavours of ginger, coriander and fish sauce.*

*Preparation time **15 minutes + 1 day marinating***
*Total cooking time **1 hour***
Serves 4

12 chicken wings
4 cloves garlic, roughly chopped
4 black peppercorns
15 g (¹/₂ oz) coriander stalks or root
1 tablespoon finely grated fresh ginger
30 ml (1 fl oz) fish sauce (nam pla)
60 ml (2 fl oz) soy sauce
60 ml (2 fl oz) honey
2 tablespoons roughly chopped coriander leaves
2 spring onions, cut lengthways into thin strips

1 Wash the chicken wings and pat dry. Tuck the tip of
each wing under the thickest part to make a triangular
shape. Place in a non-metallic bowl and set aside.
2 To make the marinade, use a pestle and mortar to
pound the garlic, peppercorns, coriander stalks and
ginger into a paste. Add the fish sauce, soy sauce and
honey and stir to combine. Pour the marinade over the
chicken wings and turn to coat. Cover the bowl with
plastic wrap and leave in the refrigerator to marinate for
24 hours.
3 Preheat the oven to hot 210°C (415°F/Gas 6–7).
Arrange the chicken wings in a shallow roasting tin in a
well-spaced single layer and pour over the marinade.
Bake for 1 hour, basting frequently, until tender.
4 Arrange the hot wings on a serving dish and garnish
with the coriander and spring onions. You may wish to
serve a dipping sauce such as chilli sauce. Provide finger
bowls and napkins as these are eaten with the fingers.

Stuffed chicken breast with celeriac purée

A perfect combination of delicate and robust flavours with a syrupy mango chutney sauce—the finished dish is even greater than the sum of its delicious parts.

Preparation time **40 minutes**
Total cooking time **1 hour**
Serves 4

STUFFING
2 chicken thighs
75 g (2¹/₂ oz) plain yoghurt
2 tablespoons chopped celery

300 g (10 oz) celeriac, peeled and chopped
few drops of lemon juice
3 tablespoons plain yoghurt
4 skinless chicken breast fillets, about 120 g (4 oz) each
1 tablespoon oil
1 tablespoon mango chutney
2 tablespoons sherry vinegar
500 ml (16 fl oz) chicken stock (see page 62)
20 g (³/4 oz) unsalted butter
2 tablespoons each of diced carrot, onion, celery and apple

1 To make the stuffing, remove the skin from the thighs and scrape the meat from the bones, reserving the bones. Weigh 200 g (6¹/2 oz) of the meat (discard any left over) and work until smooth in a food processor. Add the yoghurt, process until combined and transfer to a bowl. Add the celery and season. Mix and set aside.

2 Add the celeriac and lemon juice to a pan of boiling salted water and simmer for 20 minutes, or until the celeriac is tender. Drain, return to the pan and shake over the heat for 1 minute. Purée in a food processor with the yoghurt, season to taste and keep warm.

3 Preheat the oven to moderately hot 190°C (375°F/Gas 5). Cut a slit in the side of each chicken breast, about two thirds of the way through, and spoon in the stuffing, avoiding overfilling. Heat the oil in an ovenproof shallow pan and lightly brown the chicken breasts. Add the thigh bones to the pan and bake in the oven for 10 minutes. Remove the breasts, set aside and keep warm. Pour off the fat from the pan, then add the chutney and vinegar and cook on the stove top until syrupy. Add the stock and cook for 10 minutes, or until reduced by a third. Season to taste, strain and set aside.

4 Melt the butter in a small pan, add the carrot, onion and celery and cook gently for 5 minutes, or until softened but not coloured. Add the apple and cook for 2 minutes. Spoon the vegetables onto plates and top with the chicken breasts and sauce. Serve with the celeriac purée.

Chicken brochettes with vegetable rice

Brochette is a French word for skewer or kebab and is also the term for this method of cooking. Marinating the chicken before grilling on the skewers makes the meat more tender and flavourful.

Preparation time **30 minutes + refrigeration**
  (1 hour or overnight)
Total cooking time **1 hour**
Serves 4

4 skinless chicken breast fillets
I large red capsicum (pepper), halved and seeded
12 button mushrooms
I onion
200 ml (6¹/2 fl oz) corn oil
100 ml (3¹/4 fl oz) soy sauce
juice of I lemon
2 tomatoes
I onion, chopped
100 ml (3¹/4 fl oz) white wine vinegar
500 ml (16 fl oz) chicken stock (see page 62)
I teaspoon chopped fresh thyme
30 g (I oz) capers, rinsed and roughly chopped

VEGETABLE RICE
oil, for cooking
I onion, finely sliced
200 g (6¹/2 oz) long-grain rice
¹/2 red capsicum (pepper), diced
¹/2 green capsicum (pepper), diced
60 g (2 oz) frozen baby peas, thawed

1 Cut each chicken breast into six nuggets. Cut the capsicum into 12 rough squares. Remove and discard the mushroom stalks. Halve and then cut the onion into large pieces to match the pepper. Thread the chicken, capsicum, mushroom and onion alternately onto skewers and place in a shallow dish. Mix together the corn oil, soy sauce and lemon juice, spoon over the brochettes and baste well. Cover and refrigerate for at least 1 hour but preferably overnight.

2 To make the vegetable rice, preheat the oven to moderately hot 200°C (400°F/Gas 6). In an ovenproof casserole, heat 2–3 tablespoons oil on the stove top, add the onion and cook gently until transparent but not coloured. With a wooden spoon, stir in the rice and cook for 1 minute. Add 400 ml (12¾ fl oz) water and bring to the boil, stirring continuously. Season with salt and pepper. Cover the dish and put into the oven for 15 minutes, or until the rice is tender. Lightly mix in the red and green capsicum and the peas and season to taste. Turn the oven to very low, cover the rice and return to the oven to keep warm.

3 Bring a pan of water to the boil and score a cross in the base of each tomato. Plunge the tomatoes into the boiling water for 10 seconds, then transfer to a bowl of cold water. Peel the skin away from the cross. Quarter and seed the tomatoes, remove the stalk and roughly dice the flesh.

4 Lift the brochettes from the marinade, reserving the liquid, and grill for 4 minutes on each side, or until the chicken juices run clear when pierced with a skewer. Transfer to a tray, cover and keep warm in the oven.

5 Add the onion to the juices in the grill pan and place over low to medium heat on the stove top, stirring until lightly coloured. Pour on the vinegar and stir until reduced by half. Add the reserved marinade and cook for 2 minutes. Add the stock and cook for a further 10–15 minutes, or until reduced to a syrup. Stir in the tomato, thyme and capers and season to taste. Serve the rice and brochettes with the sauce spooned over the top.

Chef's tip The brochettes may be prepared the day before and kept in the refrigerator overnight.

Chef's techniques

◆

Trussing for roasting

Rinse the bird inside and out, then dry with paper towels. Trussing the chicken helps it keep its shape.

Use ordinary household string to truss. Tie the legs together, wrapping the string under the parson's nose first.

After the legs, take the string towards the neck of the bird, passing it down between the legs and the body.

Turn the bird over and cross the string over in the centre, underneath the wings. Wrap the string around the wings to keep them flat.

Tie the string into a knot or bow to secure the chicken wings in place. Trim off the ends of the string and the chicken is ready for roasting.

Making chicken stock

Good, flavoursome home-made stock can be the cornerstone of a great dish.

Cut up 750 g (1 1/2 lb) chicken bones and carcass and put in a pan with a roughly chopped onion, carrot and celery stick. Add 6 peppercorns, a bouquet garni and 4 litres cold water.

Bring to the boil and let the stock simmer gently for 2–3 hours, skimming off any scum that rises to the surface using a large spoon. Strain the stock through a sieve into a clean bowl, then allow to cool.

Chill the stock overnight, then lift off any fat. If you can't leave overnight, drag the surface of the hot strained stock with paper towels to lift off the fat. The stock can be refrigerated for 3 days. Makes 1.5–2 litres.

To freeze, boil the stock to reduce to 500 ml (16 fl oz). Allow to cool and freeze until solid. Transfer to a plastic bag and seal. To make 2 litres stock, add 1.5 litres water to 500 ml (16 fl oz) concentrated stock.

Jointing a chicken

The flavour of a dish will often be better if, rather than buying pieces, you cut up a whole bird.

Use a pair of kitchen scissors to cut through the length of the breastbone, then turn the chicken over and cut down either side of the backbone to completely remove it.

The backbone should come away in one piece. Then cut the bird into four pieces, following the natural contours. You can also remove the wing tips at this stage, if you wish.

For eight pieces, cut each breast in half, so one piece has the wing attached, and cut through the leg joint to separate the drumstick from the thigh.

Bouquet garni

Add the flavour and aroma of herbs to your dish with a freshly made bouquet garni.

Wrap the green part of a leek loosely around a bay leaf, a sprig of thyme, some celery leaves and a few stalks of parsley, then tie with string. Leave a long tail to the string for easy removal.

Removing the wishbone

The wishbone is found at the neck of the bird. Its removal makes carving the breast easier.

Pull back the skin from the neck cavity. Use your fingers to feel for the wishbone just inside—you may need to slit the skin a little. Cut around the wishbone with a sharp knife, then scrape the meat away.

Cut away the wishbone at the joint and lift it out.

Scraping a drumstick

The darker meat on the chicken leg has a lot of flavour and is good for terrines and stuffings.

Removing the meat from the bone can be fiddly. Pull the skin off the legs, from the fat end of the drumstick.

Hold the knuckle end of the drumstick and use a sharp knife to cut around the bone, then scrape away the flesh.

Published by Murdoch Books® a division of Murdoch Magazines Pty Limited, 213 Miller Street, North Sydney NSW 2060.

Murdoch Books and Le Cordon Bleu thank the 32 masterchefs of all the Le Cordon Bleu Schools, whose knowledge and expertise have made this book possible, especially: Chef Cliche (MOF), Chef Terrien, Chef Boucheret, Chef Duchêne (MOF), Chef Guillut, Chef Steneck, Paris; Chef Males, Chef Walsh, Chef Hardy, London; Chef Chantefort, Chef Bertin, Chef Jambert, Chef Honda, Tokyo; Chef Salembien, Chef Boutin, Chef Harris, Sydney; Chef Lawes, Adelaide; Chef Guiet, Chef Denis, Ottawa. Of the many students who helped the Chefs test each recipe, a special mention to graduates David Welch and Allen Wertheim. A very special acknowledgment to Directors Susan Eckstein, Great Britain, and Kathy Shaw, Paris, who have been responsible for the coordination of the Le Cordon Bleu team throughout this series.

Murdoch Books®
Managing Editor: Kay Halsey
Series Concept, Design and Art Direction: Juliet Cohen
Editor: Jane Price
Food Director: Jody Vassallo
Food Editors: Dimitra Stais, Tracy Rutherford
Designer: Annette Fitzgerald
Photographers: Jon Bader, Joe Filshie, Chris Jones
Food Stylists: Amanda Cooper, Carolyn Fienberg, Mary Harris
Food Preparation: Michelle Earl, Jo Forrest, Kerrie Ray
Chef's Techniques Photographer: Reg Morrison
Home Economist: Michelle Lawton

CEO & Publisher: Anne Wilson
Publishing Director: Catie Ziller
General Manager: Mark Smith
Creative Director: Marylouise Brammer
International Sales Director: Mark Newman

National Library of Australia Cataloguing-in-Publication Data
Chicken. ISBN 0 86411 737 X. 1. Cookery (Chicken). (Series: Le Cordon Bleu home collection). 641.665

Printed by Toppan Printing (S) Pte Ltd
First Printed 1997
©Design and photography Murdoch Books® 1997
©Text Le Cordon Bleu 1997
Distributed in the UK by D Services, 6 Euston Street, Freemen's Common, Leicester LE2 7SS Tel 0116-254-7671 Fax 0116-254-4670. Distributed in Canada by Whitecap (Vancouver) Ltd, 351 Lynn Avenue, North Vancouver, BC V7J 2C4 Tel 604-980-9852 Fax 604-980-8197 or Whitecap (Ontario) Ltd, 47 Coldwater Road, North York, ON M3B 1Y8 Tel 416-444-3442 Fax 416-444-6630

The Publisher and Le Cordon Bleu wish to thank Carole Sweetnam for her help with this series.
Front cover: Chicken en croûte

IMPORTANT INFORMATION

CONVERSION GUIDE

1 cup = 250 ml (8 fl oz)
1 Australian tablespoon = 20 ml (4 teaspoons)
1 UK tablespoon = 15 ml (3 teaspoons)

NOTE: We have used 20 ml tablespoons. If you are using a 15 ml tablespoon, for most recipes the difference will be negligible. For recipes using baking powder, gelatine, bicarbonate of soda and flour, add an extra teaspoon for each tablespoon specified.

CUP CONVERSIONS—DRY INGREDIENTS

1 cup flour, plain or self-raising = 125 g (4 oz)
1 cup sugar, caster = 250 g (8 oz)
1 cup breadcrumbs, dry = 125 g (4 oz)

IMPORTANT: Those who might be at risk from the effects of salmonella food poisoning (the elderly, pregnant women, young children and those suffering from immune deficiency diseases) should consult their GP with any concerns about eating raw eggs.